South Australia

A PHOTOGRAPHIC JOURNEY

South Australia

A PHOTOGRAPHIC JOURNEY NICK RAINS

NEW HOLLAND

contents

Message from the Premier of South Australia
The Hon John Olsen MP

From our world-class regions to our action-packed calendar of international events, South Australia has something for everyone. Whether you're seeking a memorable fine dining experience, the raw beauty of the Outback, or a peaceful beachside escape, you'll discover it in South Australia.

South Australia's capital, Adelaide, is a great base from which to explore the state's many attractions. Home to a wide range of museums, galleries and restaurants, Adelaide is a cultural mecca, and the setting for international events such as Tasting Australia, the International Horse Trials and the Adelaide and Fringe festivals. Adelaide is also becoming renowned as the motor sport capital of Australia through the roar and excitement of the Clipsal 500 Adelaide V8 street race and the Classic Adelaide rally.

Venturing out of the city, from the quaint towns of the Adelaide Hills, to the rugged beauty of the Flinders Ranges and the Outback, South Australia is as diverse as it is beautiful. The wine regions of the Barossa, Clare Valley and Coonawarra produce some of the world's finest wines, while the coastal towns of the south-east are renowned for their seafood and popularity as a summer holiday destination. If a holiday by the water is what you're seeking, you might consider cruising down the mighty Murray River on a houseboat, or visiting the seaside towns of the Eyre and Fleurieu peninsulas, popular for their water sports, whale watching and some of the state's best fishing spots. Kangaroo Island is a must-see destination for nature lovers and is home to numerous species of flora and fauna now extinct on the mainland. So, whether you're looking for the excitement of a car race, a world-class arts experience, or simply relaxing with good food and wine, you can find it in South Australia.

This spectacular book showcases the state's premier attractions and also provides an insight into lesser known places, and the people who inhabit them. The stunning photography accompanied by informative text reveals the many fascinating aspects of South Australia. This is a book that deserves a place on the shelves of South Australians as well as overseas and interstate visitors, and one which will, I hope, encourage you to visit our state soon and discover its many secrets.

JOHN OLSEN
Premier

NORTHERN TERRITORY

QUEENSLAND

Witjira National Park

Simpson Desert Regional Reserve

STURT STONY DESERT

SIMPSON DESERT

Innamincka Regional Reserve

○ Oodnadatta

GREAT VICTORIA DESERT

STRZELECKI DESERT

Innamincka ○

Lake Eyre

Lake Eyre National Park

WESTERN AUSTRALIA

Coober Pedy ○

Strzelecki Regional Reserve

○ Marree

QUEENSLAND

Gammon Ranges

Lake Frome

Flinders Ranges

NEW SOUTH WALES

Nullarbor Regional Reserve

Yellabinna Regional Reserve

NULLARBOR PLAIN

Woomera ○

Lake Torrens

Flinders Ranges National Park

Nullarbor National Park

Lake Gairdner National Park

Ceduna ○

Gawler Ranges

Lake Gairdner

Port Augusta ○

GREAT AUSTRALIAN BIGHT

Whyalla ○

○ Port Pirie

Cowell ○

Murray River

SPENCER GULF

Gawler ○

Coffin Bay National Park

Port Lincoln ○

Lincoln National Park

Adelaide ○

Murray Bridge ○

GULF ST VINCENT

Innes National Park

Victor Harbor

Kingscote ○

Coorong National Park

Kangaroo Island

Naracoorte ○

VICTORIA

Mount Gambier ○

Canunda National Park

SOUTHERN OCEAN

N

0   5   150km

WA

NT

QLD

SA

NSW

ACT

VIC

TAS

Introduction

Sipping a glass of fine chardonnay, gazing over endless ranks of vines marching across the rolling Barossa landscape, it is hard to imagine that most of South Australia is harsh desert and that it is the driest state in Australia. It is a place of contrasts: vivid red sands of the Simpson Desert; deep blues of the Eyre Peninsula coast; fertile greens of the Adelaide Hills; and barren and waterless wastes of the Stony Desert.

If you crave.wide open spaces, look no further than the endless Nullarbor Plain. If the dynamic cafe scene of inner city living takes your fancy, then Rundle Street in Adelaide is for you. From sandy desert to coastal dunes, from eccentric outback pubs to sophisticated city restaurants, South Australia has something to offer the most discerning of visitors.

Birth of a Model State

Australian history, after British settlement, records the earliest developments happening on the eastern coast. It was a full 209 years after the first sighting of its coastline by the Dutch ship, *Guilden Zeepard*, on 27 July 1836, that the new state of South Australia was founded. Two years later the first migrants arrived. No convicts were allowed in the fledgling settlement, making this the only Australian state populated by free citizens.

Within a year of the arrival of the first settlers, Colonel Light had surveyed the present site of Adelaide with the intention of creating a model city that would test planning theories put forward in an innovative plan: the Wakefield plan. As the authorities wished to avoid problems experienced in the older colonies, where land was affordable by almost anyone, Light's plan sought regulation of land sales and thus control of the new economy.

During the first ten years after settlement copper mines opened at Burra, and gold was discovered near Montacute. In 1847, the eleventh year, grape planting commenced in the Barossa region which has become one of the premier wine regions in the world. Representative government was established in 1850, and navigation of the Murray River, a prominent feature of Australian history, was pioneered around 1853.

Since these formative years South Australia has developed into a kind of 'best kept secret'. The residents of Adelaide, probably the best informed of all Australian city dwellers when it comes to their heritage and history, swear they could live nowhere else. The Adelaide Arts Festival is one of the most important events on the Australian cultural calendar, and the tourism industry is ever-increasing as people come to explore the wild regions of the state.

Unspoiled Scenery

Whilst South Australia cannot boast drawcards like Kakadu, Uluru and the Great Barrier Reef, it does have a wealth of important and attractive places to visit. Some people even say that the popularity of famous places is a big turn-off, and that they prefer quieter and more unspoilt places to visit. Whalers Way, near Port Lincoln at the tip of the Eyre Peninsula, is an example of such a place. The coastline is as wild and rugged as the best parts of the more famous

Western Australian southern coast. Blowholes send up 30-metre-high plumes of spray, and 100-metre cliffs tower over seal-inhabited bays of the deepest blue imaginable. Yet, in spite of all this glory, when I visited to shoot the pictures for this book, I saw only one other car all day.

Another of South Australia's secret spots can be found not far off the road near Penong. There are sand dunes and beaches to rival the best in any state, yet apart from those 'in the know', no-one stops to visit. It would seem that a great many travellers pass straight through South Australia, heading for Western Australia, across the Nullarbor Plain. So focused are they on the huge distances ahead, that they don't stop to look at the special places they are passing.

South Australia is also home to one of Australia's most significant fossil finds, within the spectacular World Heritage listed caves at Naracoorte. The fossils of prehistoric animals date from around the time of the earliest inhabitants of the country and give a fascinating insight into the world 50 000 years ago.

Surprising Facts

Statistics about South Australia's weather reveal some surprising facts. It is the driest of all Australian states with 80 per cent of its area getting less than 250mm of rain per year. To give some idea of what this means, a wild storm in Brisbane can deliver more rain than this in a single day. Adelaide receives about 600mm annually which makes for a pleasant dry climate without the draining summer humidity of cities like Sydney and Brisbane. In the south, temperatures rarely rise over the 40°C mark, although in northern deserts this is close to the average temperature.

Australia is known as an urbanised nation and South Australia demonstrates this more than any other state. 99 per cent of its population lives south of the 32nd parallel (a line which passes through Ceduna and Broken Hill). In addition to this, of the state's 1.4 million inhabitants, more than 1 million live in Adelaide (1994 statistics). Visitors to the northern deserts are often surprised by the lack of people in these vast areas. Most desert towns marked on maps have under 1000 residents, and some, like William Creek, only four!

The south-east parts of South Australia are well-populated, well-watered and produce most of the state's wine. In addition to the Barossa, there are many equally fine wine growing districts, including: the Coonawarra near Penola; McLaren Vale near Adelaide; and the Clare Valley just north of Adelaide. Scattered around the rest of the state from Renmark to Kingston SE are small pockets of land where significant amounts of grapes are grown. The state's prodigious wine industry produces 40 per cent of the total Australian output, all from 12 per cent of Australia's area!

Gems for the Visitor

Any preconceived notions about what to expect when visiting South Australia are likely to be way off the mark. Most visits are far too short to investigate the unexpected experiences each of the state's regions has to offer. Once these treasures are discovered, even the veteran traveller will want to explore just one more road, or head off to just one more beach. Furthermore, every town seems to have a little gem in store for the visitor, whether it be a breathtaking view, an unspoilt beach, a heritage building or a fine restaurant.

Adelaide & the Adelaide Hills

Adelaide, with its wide tree-lined avenues and generous encircling parklands, is a pleasant change from the contemporary motor-vehicle-driven approaches to town-planning which often result in clogged freeways and inner city grid-locks. The city has an open feeling and while there are the usual log-jams of traffic during rush-hour, there is never a sense of being hemmed in.

The orderly arrangement of roads and parks is due to Adelaide's long formal city administration, dating back to 1836, in the days of Colonel Light. Early administrators were so focused on bringing to life a radical city blueprint, based on ideas dating back to Roman times, that it took 24 years to build a grand administration headquarters. These dedicated men put together a new city from scratch, free from the historical design baggage that dogged other, older settlements.

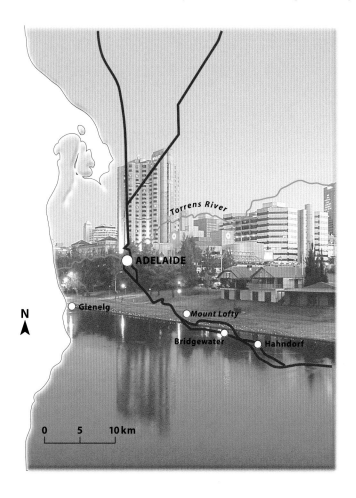

Adelaide is Australia's fifth largest city with a population of just over 1 million people. The sea breeze from the coast, just 5 kilometres away, moderates the worst of the summer heat. The surrounding hills districts provide an escape to the wooded parks and gardens of the Mount Lofty Ranges, where residential sprawl has been successfully held in check, and picturesque vineyards are tucked away amoungst the rolling green hills.

The heart of the city is around King William Street Bridge where the Festival Centre, Adelaide Oval, Casino and Elder Park sit looking out over the Torrens River. North Terrace, running parallel to the river, is the administrative hub of Adelaide and the north side of the street is dominated by the Railway Station, Parliament House, Government House, Art Gallery of South Australia, Adelaide Hospital and University—all imposing examples of Victorian architecture.

In keeping with Adelaide's reputation as a major sponsor of the arts, the gardens and pathways around the Art Gallery are dotted with modern sculptures ranging from huge taps jutting out from the tearoom's wall to a series of fish swimming through a courtyard gate. The Adelaide Arts Festival, held every other year, is a huge event on the calendar with performers from all over the country converging on the Festival Centre, showing off street theatre, acting and music to the thousands of visitors who come here at Easter.

One block back from the river, just south of North Terrace, is the thriving commercial centre, emanating from Rundle Street Mall. This is where all the best shops and arcades can be found. Together with the adjacent Hindley Street, this part of town also pulses with life after the shops close, when bars and restaurants open their doors. Evening is a good time to be out and about in Adelaide as the most popular parts of town, with a choice of excellent restaurants, can be just as busy as at lunchtime.

Victoria Square, with its magnificent fountain and grand old Post Office, is also the terminus for the 1929 trams which weave through traffic, to the coast, and drop off passengers right next to the beach in the seaside resort of Glenelg. Here grand old Victorian homes, facing magnificent long beaches, are a reminder of the days when Glenelg was a thriving seaside retreat for the wealthy. Today, it is a popular spot for a cappuccino and a Greek salad.

Mount Lofty is the dominant hill in the encircling Adelaide Hills. Perched right on top is the Mount Lofty Summit Restaurant. A spectacular panoramic view of the city, displayed in twinkling lights on the vast plain below, can be enjoyed over a fine dinner. This, together with the extensive Mount Lofty Botanic Gardens not far away, should be on the top of any 'to do' list for visitors to this state.

So close to the city but a world apart in atmosphere, the Adelaide Hills are a sanctuary for residents and visitors alike especially in the summer months when many people come to take advantage of the cooler air. Rolling hills, winding roads and tiny villages are a reminder of days gone, when the pace was slower, and more people lived off the land. Tiny hamlets like Piccadilly, Crafers and Bridgewater are places modern development has passed by. Many of their beautifully restored original buildings are still in use.

Hahndorf, only a half-hour's drive from Adelaide, has turned its ambience, created through the evident influence of the early German settlers, into a successful tourist destination now preserved as a state heritage area. Originally, local Aboriginals knew the spot as 'bukartilla' meaning 'swimming place', however German settlers, who set up their farms here in 1839, renamed the village Hahndorf (meaning Hahn's town) after Dirk Hahn, the captain of their ship. Today, most of the shops in the tree-lined main street have been fully restored to their original German character, and various bakeries and tearooms sell apfelstrudel and Black Forest gateau alongside lamingtons and cappuccinos.

ABOVE: The Bicentennial Conservatory in the Botanic Gardens is the largest glass-house in Australia, and houses a complete rainforest environment.

RIGHT: St Peter's Cathedral, North Adelaide, was built between 1869 and 1876 in French Gothic Revival style.

BOTTOM RIGHT: King William Street, the city's main thorough-fare, looking towards North Terrace. Leafy streets such as this are a characteristic feature of Adelaide.

OPPOSITE: The Adelaide Festival Centre complex was completed in 1977 and is situated close to the Torrens River. The gardens are a popular spot for a picnic.

PAGES 10 AND 11: The city skyline of Adelaide seen from North Adelaide.

ABOVE LEFT: Adelaide Fruit and Produce Exchange on East Terrace dates from 1903, and has been fully restored after a period of disuse. The plaster frieze depicts fruit, vegetables and wheat.

ABOVE RIGHT: Sculptures are to be found in the most unlikely places around the Art Gallery. Here, a fish swims through a courtyard gate.

LEFT: Adelaide Arcade is one of several arcades radiating off Rundle Mall, the main shopping area in the city centre.

RIGHT: This fruit and vegetable stall in Rundle Mall displays a variety of the excellent fresh produce that is readily available.

TOP: Quirky modern art is a distinctive feature of the Art Gallery grounds. These giant taps protrude from the wall of the gallery's tearoom.

ABOVE LEFT: Detail of the ornate Victorian bandstand in Elder Park, on the banks of the Torrens River. Brass bands play here on Sunday mornings.

ABOVE RIGHT: The casino overlooks the unusual abstract patterns and shapes of the 1970s Festival Centre Plaza.

LEFT: The statue of 'Light's Vision' stands atop Montefiore Hill, where Colonel Light is said to have stood and mapped out the first city plan. Now, the statue overlooks the modern city skyline.

RIGHT: Government House on North Terrace is Adelaide's oldest public building. It was completed in 1855 and has been home to every governor except the first.

ABOVE: At night, Rundle Street comes to life with trendy cafes and fine restaurants.

RIGHT: Adelaide Zoo is very involved with preserving the rare Yellow-footed Rock Wallaby and has a fine exhibit of these endangered animals.

ABOVE: The trams that make the half-hour trip to the suburban seaside resort of Glenelg are Adelaide icons. Red leather seats and wood-panelling are part of the original fixtures and fittings.

ABOVE: Port Adelaide has some of the best preserved examples of Colonial architecture in Australia, and retains the atmosphere of a busy shipping port.

OPPOSITE: Flanking Adelaide to the south and east are the Adelaide Hills, where many fine vineyards are tucked away amongst the rolling hills and valleys.

LEFT: Old Government House is set in the beautiful surrounds of Belair Recreational Park, to the south of the city.

BOTTOM LEFT: The up-market suburb of North Adelaide is an easy stroll from the city centre, and features quiet leafy streets and many interesting buildings.

LEFT AND ABOVE: Hahndorf is a popular day trip from the city. Settled in 1839, this quiet village has been fully restored to its original German heritage. The German Arms Hotel (above) is the main focus of the street and is a great place to watch the world go by on a hot summer's day. Elsewhere, shops sell local crafts, German breads and apfelstrudel while a museum in the Hahndorf Academy has exhibits on the heritage of the area.

FOLLOWING PAGES: The Eden Valley is the Barossa's lesser known wine-producing cousin and lies directly to the south-east between Angaston and Eden Valley village.

Wine Regions of South Australia

South Australia produces slightly under half of all the wine made in the whole of Australia and just about all the different wine styles can be found on South Australian labels—shiraz, semillon, chardonnay, cabernet sauvignon, riesling, muscat, fortified, grenache and mourvèdre. In addition to the well known regions such as the Barossa Valley, Clare Valley, McLaren Vale and Coonawarra, there are many other places producing fine wines, such as Cape Jaffa, Langhorne Creek, Mount Gambier, Mount Benson, Padthaway and the southern Eyre Peninsula. With so many styles and locations, the sheer variety of tastes to be found in South Australia

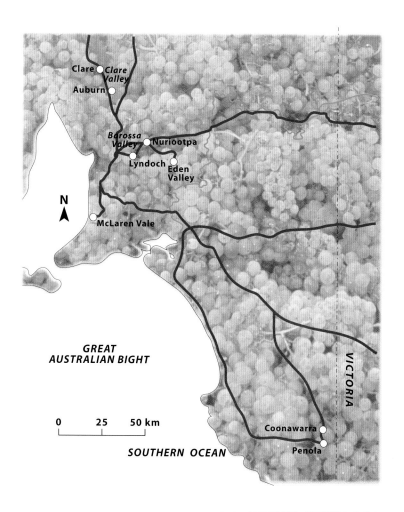

is quite remarkable—there is no such thing as a plain 'South Australian wine'.

About halfway between the mighty Murray River and Adelaide are the world famous wine growing towns and valleys collectively known as the Barossa. This area, unique in Australia, has a distinctive German heritage, traditional festivals and above all, some of the best wines in the world. In 1837, after glowing reports about the region from German minerologist Johann Menge, the ubiquitous Colonel Light named the district after the Battle of Barrosa in Spain, between the English and the French. This contemporary spelling has somehow evolved into the modern version, Barossa.

Initially, in 1838, a group of Lutherans settled in Bethany. They were followed by other German groups and groups of middle-class English settlers who aspired to the life of the 'country gentleman'. This cultural mix has provided the unique style of the area which seems to have acquired the best aspects of both cultures. This, in turn, has lead to the great success of the region.

Today, along the main road through the townships of Lyndoch, Tanunda and Nuriootpa, you will find vineyard signs for the famous labels supplied by city wine merchants: Yalumba, Seppelts, Jacob's Creek, Peter Lehman and Bethany, to name just a few. These are household names amongst wine drinkers all over the country, and in some cases all over the world.

The Barossa is far more European in style than other Australian wine districts, due not only to its cultural roots, but also to the geography of the region. Small vineyards, planted to take advantage of variations in drainage, soil type and aspect, have allowed many different types of grapes to be grown and different styles of viticulture to be practised. The Barossa is best known for its fine shiraz wines, but equally popular these days are semillons, chardonnays and rieslings as well as cabernets, grenaches and mourvèdres. Some wineries produce excellent fortified wines as well. For visitors, this means that the variety and scope of local winetasting, at over 40 wineries, is almost endless. Weekend trips from the city have become an institution for Adelaide residents and tourists alike.

The Barossa and Eden valleys are not all wineries and drinking however. The region has much to offer in the way of culture and heritage. Every two years at Easter, the Barossa Vintage Festival attracts visitors from all over the country, as well as from overseas, to an extensive series of concerts, fairs, markets, picnics and demonstrations which make up one of the most important festivals in the South Australian calendar. The heritage value of the region is as interesting as the wines to most visitors. With German settlers moving into the region so soon after the state was founded, there is an unbroken link with early post-settlement history. Many buildings in the area are still used for the trades and crafts practised in them 160 years ago.

A short distance south of Adelaide, and now almost an outer district of the city, is the wine growing region of McLaren Vale. This region is slightly nearer to Adelaide than the Barossa and, with its rolling hills and historic vineyards, has become equally popular with wine-loving visitors and locals alike for its distinctive full-flavoured reds and whites. There are over 50 wineries here ranging from big operations like Seaview and Hardy's to smaller, family-run ones like Kay's.

Another household name amongst wines is the Coonawarra district around Penola in the south-east of the state where the local speciality is fine cabernet sauvignons. This very specific area, only about 12 kilometres by 2 kilometres, is packed with wineries like Leconfield, Wynn's, Rymill's and Rouge Homme to name just a few. Coonawarra is also one of the oldest wine growing districts in Australia and John Riddoch is credited with starting the local industry over 100 years ago—his original winery is now Wynn's Coonawarra Estate.

If you like rieslings then you can't go too far wrong with any label from the Clare Valley, an hour or so north of Adelaide. Winemaking here dates back even further than the Coonawarra to the mid-19th century and today family-run operations like Jim Barry turn out great wines year after year.

ABOVE LEFT: This old wine press near Kapunda is one of the biggest presses ever built.

ABOVE MIDDLE AND RIGHT: Seppelts Winery in Seppeltsfield has been fully restored to its original glory. The beautiful heritage setting makes the wines taste even better!

OPPOSITE: The Keg Factory in the Barossa makes wine kegs the old-fashioned way and supplies casks to many of the local wineries.

ABOVE LEFT AND RIGHT: Late in the season, the best of the grapes are picked by hand at Jim Barry Wines in the Clare Valley. Fewer grapes are damaged this way allowing the winery's best wines to be made.

ABOVE: Rockford Wines in the Barossa show off their traditional wine-making, where huge wooden vats stained with years of use are filled and pressed by hand.

FOLLOWING PAGES: Chateau Tanunda is one of the most distinctive wineries in the Barossa and is right next to Tanunda itself.

LEFT AND OPPOSITE: Built in 1880, Yallum Park was the home of John Riddoch, the founder of the Coonawarra wine industry. The house is almost entirely original inside with hand-painted wallpaper and glass shipped from England. It is open to visitors.

LEFT: Brands Winery in the Coonawarra district is still operated by the original family —Eric Brand has one of the most extensive personal wine collections in the country.

OPPOSITE: The cellar of Hardy's Tintara Winery in McLaren Vale makes an appropriate setting for tasting the local product.

RIGHT: The view south towards Willunga stretches over the rolling ranks of grapevines, from a vantage point on Osborne Road.

BOTTOM LEFT: Some of the homesteads in the McLaren Vale district have a distinct Tuscan style to them.

BOTTOM RIGHT: McLaren Vale is home to some of the best known names in Australian wine.

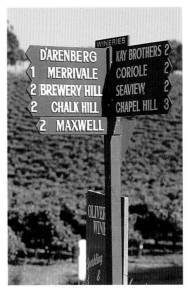

LEFT AND OPPOSITE: Held every two years, the Barossa Vintage Festival has no equal when it comes to celebrating the end of all the hard work of harvest time. The towns of Angaston, Nuriootpa and Tanunda host all sorts of events over the Festival week, from scarecrow competitions to Barber Shop Quartets, and from village craft fetes to traditional costumes.

LEFT: The distinctive main entrance to Chateau Yaldara with its sweeping staircase looking out over manicured gardens.

FOLLOWING PAGES: The Sleaford sand dunes front the wild coastline of Lincoln National Park.

Eyre Peninsula & the West

The Peninsula

The slogan,' A Breath of Fresh Eyre', on the tourism brochure for the Eyre Peninsula region, sums it up perfectly. This part of South Australia is commonly overlooked by travellers, minds set on reaching Western Australia as they whisk past on the Eyre Highway. It is a pity because the Eyre Peninsula offers some of the most interesting places in the state to visit, a refreshing change from the more popular areas in the south-east.

The peninsula stretches from Whyalla, the second biggest town in the state, west to the state border, some 1000 kilometres away. North to south this region covers 400 kilometres from the Gawler Ranges to the tip of Cape Carnot on Whalers Way, and Cape Catastrophe in Lincoln National Park. Along both east and west coasts small fishing villages such as Cowell, Tumby Bay, Elliston and Streaky Bay are scattered, while north of the Eyre Highway the Gawler Ranges separate rural regions from the vast open spaces around Lake Gairdner.

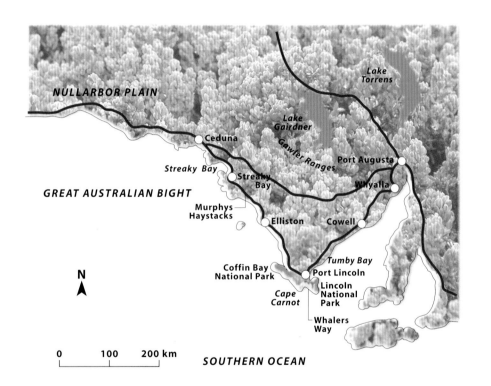

Whyalla is best known for its part in the state's huge steel industry. It has a vast steelworks which processes ore from the Iron Knob mines 50 kilometres away. Worlds away from the peace and quiet of the rest of the region, steelworks tours are nevertheless a 'must see'. Visitors are certain to be overwhelmed by the scale of the operations here.

The town is not all furnaces and conveyor belts. Whyalla has a brand new marina providing access to some excellent coastal fishing spots; the Tanderra Building houses one of the largest '00' scale model railways in the country with over 609 metres of track; there is a fine sanctuary set amongst big old myall trees displaying snakes, lizards, koalas, wallabies and birds; and the Mount Laura Homestead Museum.

Port Lincoln, the main town in the south of the peninsula, serves as a base for visitors to Lincoln National Park, Whalers Way and Coffin Bay National Park. The town itself has plenty to offer, such as the Axel Stenross Maritime Museum, but it is the spectacular local scenery that most people come to see.

Probably least known, but arguably the best part of the coastline is the Whalers Way, a self guided trip that follows huge cliffs at the southern tip of the peninsula. A key is available, for a small fee, from the Visitor Centre in Port Lincoln and the entrance to the drive is only a short way south of town, near the beautiful beach at Fishery Bay. The name 'Whalers Way' came from the small whaling operation that operated here from 1837–41. Thirty men and three boats based here waited for Southern Right Whales to pass close to shore., although the operation was only moderately successful.

The area is now a declared historic reserve with dramatic cliffs, seal colonies, the rugged shoreline and spectacular blowholes at Cape Carnot. Also near the Cape are a series of overhangs and caves known as the Whalers Grotto. Here a precarious scramble along the rocky shore leads to a huge overhung cliff where, at the back, a tunnel leads to a low but wide cave with crystal clear pools and windows in the rock, looking out over surging waves. This adventure is not for the faint-hearted but the display of the sheer power of the sea and the unusual location make it one of the best 'secret spots' around.

The West

On the way to Ceduna via the west coast, the road leads past another of the peninsula's little known places: weird red and grey rocky outcrops known as Murphys Haystacks. Situated about halfway between Port Kenny and Streaky Bay these unusual rock formations are technically called Inselbergs and are formed by differential erosion of the granite layers beneath. Although these rocks are on private land, the local landowner has set up access tracks and only asks for a donation of a couple of dollars at the gate. This helps with upkeep of the paths and is based on an honesty system.

The last major stop begins the trek to Western Australia. It is the seaside town of Ceduna, past which the road heads off into the vastness of the Nullarbor Plain. A little after Ceduna, near Penong, is a place famous with surfers but not with visitors in general. The 22 kilometre road to Point Sinclair skirts enormous white sand dunes and broad salt lakes on its way to one of the best surfing beaches in Australia—Cactus Beach. Here the legendary 'perfect break' is frequently found.

West past Ceduna, the Eyre Highway runs close to the coast which gradually changes from endless white sand dunes and beaches to soaring cliffs. In places, the limestone rock shelf at the edge of the Nullarbor Plain drops 100 metres into the vivid blue waters of the Great Australian Bight.

ABOVE: This remote holiday cottage in Lincoln National Park has views over the bay towards Port Lincoln.

LEFT: Reflected in the window of the Cowell Commercial Hotel is the quiet town of Cowell on the east coast—home to Australia's only commercial jade operation. The local jade deposits are among the largest in the world and form boulders of several tonnes each.

ABOVE AND RIGHT: Whyalla is one of the largest towns in the region with a population of about 25000. Better known for its huge BHP operations, the town also has a new marina and its maritime museum is one of the state's best.

BELOW: These unusual barns are scattered along the east coast of the Eyre Peninsula.

ABOVE: Crab pots wait on the
dock at the new marina at Lincoln
Cove, where one of Australia's
largest fishing fleets is based.

ABOVE: The commercial wharf
in Port Lincoln is a great spot to
throw in a line when the fishing
boats are out at sea.

OPPOSITE TOP: Whalers Way is a
privately owned road along the
wild coastline to the southern-
most tip of the Eyre Peninsula.

OPPOSITE BOTTOM: Fishery Bay at
the start of the Whalers Way drive.

OPPOSITE: Near Port Kenny on the west coast are the strange rock formations collectively known as Murphys Haystacks. The rocks are in fact 1500 million year old inselbergs formed by differential erosion of the granite layers beneath.

TOP RIGHT: The northern parts of this region are mostly inhospitable and the ruin of Poondara Homestead, in the Gawler Ranges, is a poignant symbol of unfulfilled dreams.

MIDDLE RIGHT: Many of the buildings in Elliston have been turned into works of art with these detailed murals.

BOTTOM RIGHT: Late in the summer months the white bottlebrush trees bloom with their distinctive flowers.

ABOVE: Cactus Beach near Penola has some of the best surf breaks in the country.

LEFT: Eucla, in the depths of the Nullarbor Plain, is known not only for its position on one of the world's loneliest roads but also for this signpost, made famous in countless photographs.

OPPOSITE: Along the Nullarbor Plain are the huge cliffs of the Great Australian Bight, looking south towards Antarctica.

ABOVE: Between Penola and Cactus Beach are extensive salt pans. At dawn, it is sometimes hard to separate the sky from the water.

ABOVE: Lake Gairdner has taken over from Lake Eyre for land speed record attempts. The hard packed white salt is perfect for speed trials, although the lake is now a national park.

FOLLOWING PAGES: Red sand dunes stretch as far as the eye can see on the western edges of the Strzelecki Desert.

The Outback

A lonely beer truck sits motionless, up to its axles in mud, in the middle of the narrow Coober Pedy–William Creek track. The driver seems pretty relaxed all things considered, after all he has been stuck there for only 24 hours. His vital mission, the delivery of hundreds of cases of beer to William Creek, has been successfully accomplished just in time for the weekend's race meeting.

The residents of William Creek, amused to hear that the beer truck is still stuck, know that someone in Coober Pedy will fix it up. They have more important things to attend to. William Creek's Race Weekend, held every year just before Easter, is the big event on the calendar around these parts. The tiny settlement on

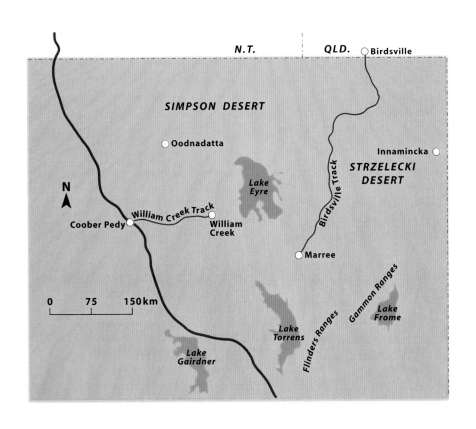

Anna Creek Station swells a hundredfold, from about four to over 400, as people come from nearby stations and from interstate to take part in an event which is half-serious (horse racing) and half-fun (beer drinking and strange games). From the publican's point of view, it is all serious. This weekend is big, not only for the pub takings, but also as a fund raiser for the Royal Flying Doctor Service. Horses are auctioned for a day; prize money is donated; and everyone puts 10 bucks 'in the pot', just to be there.

The Outback, the Red Centre, the Back of Bourke, call it what you will, its huge distances, dusty roads and isolation all make up a uniquely Australian environment. Its landscapes are different, its animals different and its people different, too. Where else would you find a delivery truck driver more relieved that the beer had got through on time, than worried about the inconvenience of being bogged for a whole day on what is supposed to be a main road in the heart of South Australia?

The outback of South Australia is considered to be just about anywhere north of the Eyre and Barrier highways, roughly along the 32nd parallel. This enormous area is one of the driest parts of Australia and includes such famous places as Lake Eyre, the Simpson Desert, the Flinders and Gammon ranges, as well as frontier towns like Oodnadatta, Coober Pedy and Innamincka. The main north-south road, the Stuart Highway, has only been sealed within the last 20 years. All other roads are clay or gravel.

Rain, although infrequent, causes havoc for a few days but tends to be pretty patchy. It is quite possible for one road to be out for a week, whilst others nearby are their usual dusty selves. Lakes marked on maps fill only every ten years or so, and then only in response to the Queensland weather, as Cooper Creek takes water from the flooding Barcoo and Thompson rivers.

Barren it may be, but the outback is not lacking in riches. Coober Pedy produces a large proportion of the world's opals, although the title of 'largest producer' is probably claimed by Mintabie, a few hundred kilometres to the north. In the east of the state, the Moomba Gas Fields supply natural gas to Adelaide and Sydney, and oil is pumped from under the Strzelecki Track. Tourism is another increasingly important resource for the outback economy. Adventure seekers from other states, and overseas visitors looking for the 'total Australian experience', come here for the vast spaces and the sense of being in the real outback. They are not disappointed.

Crossing the Simpson Desert is one of the classic journeys of central Australia. The French Line, as it is known, from Mount Dare to Birdsville is the most direct route. Most people tackle it west to east as the prevailing winds make the eastern slopes of sand dunes steeper. This may sound a bit pedantic, but given that there is a sandhill to cross every 500 metres or so, and that the trip covers over 500 kilometres, that is over 1000 potential problems to overcome, and every bit of assistance counts out here.

The Ranges

Closer to civilisation, but equally rugged, are the mighty ramparts of the Flinders and Gammon ranges. The latter are tough going and are strictly four-wheel-drive only, but the Flinders Ranges can be enjoyed, with care, in a conventional vehicle. This gives a taste of the outback in a spectacular setting of deep canyons, sweeping ridges and prolific wildlife.

The ranges and the outback of South Australia are not places to be taken lightly. You should carry extra water at all times. That said, these areas are some of the most exciting to visit. Wide open spaces and freedom of the deserted roads give one of the great experiences of this huge country. If you search here for the 'spirit of the outback' you are unlikely to be disappointed.

OPPOSITE: Towering River Red Gums create a natural archway in Parachilna Gorge as the road repeatedly crosses the river.

ABOVE: The distinctive folds of the Flinders Ranges and Wilpena Pound are seen here from the top of the China Wall, not far from Blinman.

OPPOSITE: Arkaba Woolshed is surrounded by superb Flinders Ranges scenery. Now restored, the woolshed offers camping, trail-riding and cottage accommodation.

RIGHT: Bunyeroo Gorge and the mountains beyond are one of the most distinctive scenes of the Flinders Ranges.

BOTTOM RIGHT: This sadly neglected homestead stands among stately gum trees overlooked by the high buttresses of Wilpena Pound. The building is not as old as might be imagined—it was in fact built for a period television drama.

ABOVE: With the winter air temperature hovering around freezing, the 37°C water in Dalhousie Springs, at the western edge of the Simpson Desert, makes for a luxurious early morning bath.

OPPOSITE: Even in the inhospitable red sands of the Simpson Desert, hardy plants manage to survive.

THIS PAGE: Ralph Tyler (top left) and Janelle Lugge (bottom left) prepare for a great night of music and dance. The Curdimurka Outback Ball is held every two years at a restored railway siding, once part of the Old Ghan. Over 4000 people turn up to this black tie event and party the night away under the desert stars.

OPPOSITE TOP: The Oodnadatta Track is frequented by all kinds of vehicles, none stranger than this camel wagon. There is no hurry around here—the owner often naps in the back and lets the four camels wander down the road, pulling the wagon at their own pace.

OPPOSITE BOTTOM: The Pink Roadhouse in Oodnadatta is a welcome sight for travellers in the dusty outback.

ABOVE: An old Ghan loco-motive, which once travelled the infamous route from Alice Springs to Adelaide, sits derelict at the station in Maree.

LEFT: Crossing the Simpson Desert is still a considerable challenge to the adventurous four-wheel-drive tourer. The French Line crosses dune after dune with deep, soft sand waiting for the unwary.

ABOVE: Bore water is the vital life blood of remote outback cattle stations. Tilcha Bore currently flows free and has created a large permanent wetland inhabited by migratory and native birds.

LEFT: The hot water is often used for other, more practical purposes as well!

ABOVE LEFT AND LEFT: Coober Pedy is known as an eccentric town and Crocodile Harry's is no exception with odd sculptures and an underground home full of memorabilia of Harry's eventful outback life.

ABOVE: The Breakaways near Coober Pedy show the huge variety of desert colours after a rare autumn storm has passed through. Erosion has exposed sands and rocks to form high 'jump-ups' and the views across the desert are breathtaking.

OPPOSITE: Opal mining is the reason for Coober Pedy's existence. The landscape around town suggests the presence of mighty ants, but it is the blowers of opal miners like Jon James that make the distinctive white mounds (seen here in the background) as they suck out the waste like giant vacuum cleaners.

ABOVE LEFT: John Reeves holds a locally mined opal, valued at $65000.

ABOVE RIGHT: Underground homes are the answer to the searing desert heat—the temperature stays pleasantly cool even during a scorching 45°C day.

RIGHT: The Catacomb Church is one of Coober Pedy's most famous underground buildings.

ABOVE: Innamincka trading post and hotel are situated right next to the mighty Cooper Creek in north-east South Australia. The only other building here, the old Inland Mission hospital, was abandoned for many years but has now been reopened as a National Parks headquarters.

LEFT: Emus are very common in Corner Country and can be very inquisitive. This one came up to the car, attracted by the sound of a rustling newspaper.

OPPOSITE TOP: The tales of the old mail run and the hardships of life on the cattle stations along the endless Birdsville Track have become part of Australian folklore.

OPPOSITE BOTTOM: Much of South Australia is littered with abandoned stone buildings, like this one near Hawker.

ABOVE AND OPPOSITE: William Creek, possibly the smallest town in Australia, has its own pub, racecourse and not a lot else. Once a year, however, hundreds of people from all over the state converge here for the annual Gymkhana. The Saturday events mostly involve beer, but on Sunday the serious racing begins, including the Camel Cup and various campdraft events.

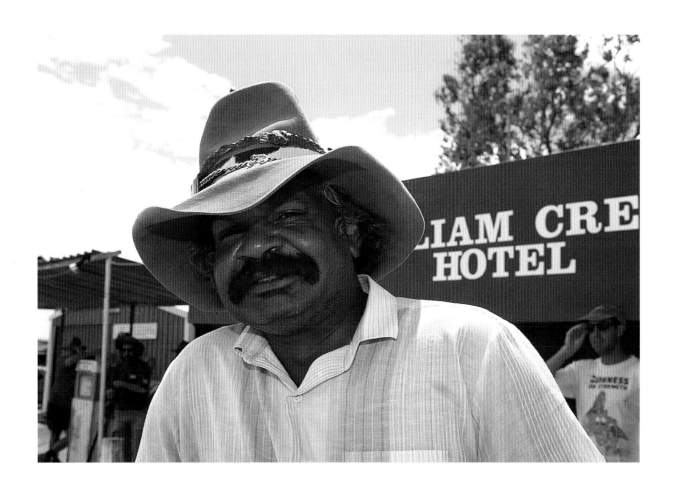

THIS PAGE AND OPPOSITE: The Gymkhana weekend is a true community event—even the local police turn up. It's also a family affair and everyone brings their children who enjoy meeting other kids they may not have seen since last year.

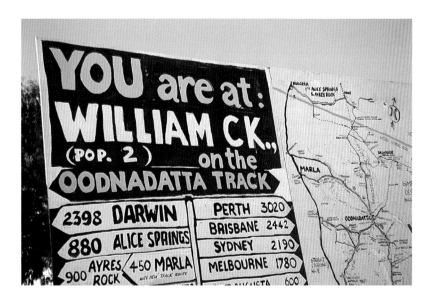

FOLLOWING PAGES: Naracoorte Caves are one of Australia's World Heritage sites, not only because of their natural splendour but also for the rich fossil deposits currently being researched there.

The River

The sight of the huge three storey *Murray Princess* paddlesteamer, churning her way past the ochre cliffs of the Murray River, is almost like a scene from the deep south of the USA. There, huge paddle steamers just like this one, plied their trade up and down the mighty Mississippi River, providing transport for goods and entertainment for passengers. Today, the *Murray Princess* provides entertainment as a floating hotel and takes guests on week-long luxury trips from Mannum up to Morgan and back.

The Murray River, known as the River Murray in South Australia, is the second longest river in the country at over 2500 kilometres in length. Combined with its major tributary, the Darling River in NSW, this river system, at 5300 kilometres, is one of the longest in the world—about eighth on the list.

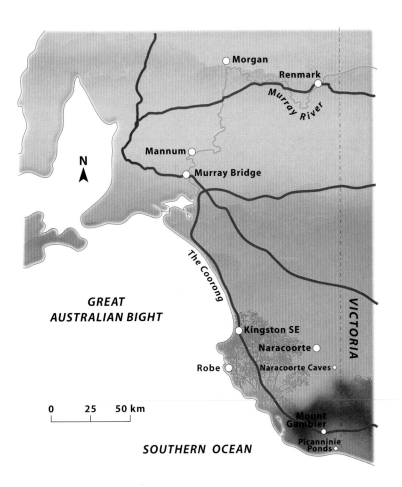

The Murray has been of vital importance to the economy of the country since its discovery by Sturt on his 1829–30 expedition, when he traced the river to its outflow near the present town of Goolwa. It was this discovery that finally put to rest the speculation about an inland sea at the heart of the continent, and was essentially responsible for the first settlements in South Australia, a few years later.

Paddlesteamers eventually became a vital link between the Eastern states and the new state of South Australia, easily arrying goods and passengers over the vast distances involved. Many towns became thriving inland ports and in places like Murray Bridge, Morgan, and Renmark old docks and wharves are still in use today. Eventually railways took over the trade, and paddlesteamers faded into history, only to be resurrected as tourist attractions in recent years.

As a source of water however, the Murray still has a vital role to play. Most of Adelaide's water is piped from the river. And with its very healthy citrus and grape growing industry the Riverland region around Renmark and Loxton is a very fertile part of the state.

The South-east

If you are tempted by a beach that is 145 kilometres long and so deserted that you will not see another living soul all day, then the Coorong in the south-east of South Australia is for you. The Coorong is a series of long narrow lagoons protected by mighty coastal dunes making up the Younghusband Peninsula, which stretches from the mouth of the Murray River all the way to Salt Creek, about 80 kilometres from Kingston. Its shallow, protected waters are home to over 150 species of water birds.

Mount Gambier, a large town of over 20000 residents, is the main centre of the south-east region. Its locally quarried white stone buildings are set amongst an intriguing landscape of extinct volcanic crater lakes. During a few days in November, one of these—the famous Blue Lake—changes colour from a dull grey to the most vivid shade of blue imaginable. Far bluer, it seems, than the sky reflected in it.

The geology of the region has some surprises in store as well. Formed of limestone, it is riddled with caves and underground waterways. Not far from Mount Gambier are the Picaninnie Ponds where the clarity of the water attracts qualified cave divers from all over the world.

Naracoorte, north of the famous Coonawarra wine district, has other sorts of cave. These have been successfully developed with visitors in mind. Naracoorte Caves Conservation Park, along with Riversleigh in Queensland, is listed amongst Australia's World Heritage sites and is very well set up with the new Wonambi Visitor Centre and hi-tech equipment for watching the activities of the Bent-Wing Bat in the Bat Cave. You can also see fossils, and spectacular limestone formations in caves where huge numbers of delicate stalactites hang in clusters from the roof.

On the coast, east of Naracoorte, is the little fishing village of Robe. In 1846 it was one of the largest ports in South Australia. The old 1863 Customs House perched above the perfect circular harbour must be one of the smallest ever built. It has been restored and has become one of the most recognisable landmarks of the town. Much of Robe's heritage has been preserved and the main street is almost completely made up of heritage buildings. This gives the town a sense of solidity, emphasising its strong link with the past.

Robe has been a holiday destination for 150 years. Today, at the height of the season, the population can rise from 900 to 9000. Outside the holiday period however is a different story—Robe is the quintessential sleepy fishing village where fishing boats are gone with the dawn. The only hustle and bustle is when they return full of lobsters for the local seafood shops.

ABOVE LEFT: The Murray River is lined with magnificent gum trees with bark patterns that resemble the flowing water of the river.

ABOVE RIGHT AND RIGHT: The river acts as a main road for hundreds of pleasure craft. The *Murray Princess*, the largest paddle-steamer still operating, adds a touch of luxury to the natural beauty of the river.

ABOVE: Quiet billabongs along the river course act as magnets for huge numbers of birds of many different species.

RIGHT AND FAR RIGHT: Loxton, in the fertile Murray valley, has preserved many old buildings from around the area in an historical village. The interiors of these old shops (opposite top and right) have been restored with all the original merchandise, and the woolshed (opposite bottom) is set up with sorting table and wool press.

BELOW: Hay bales seem to stretch as far as the eye can see in the wheat-growing areas of Swan Reach and Blanchetown.

LEFT: Looking like a giant matchstick, a post marks the way to the ocean beach over the white dunes of the Coorong.

BELOW: Pelicans in vast numbers inhabit the still waters of the Coorong lagoons.

OPPOSITE TOP: These dunes protect the inner lagoon from the effects of the ocean surf and form a narrow peninsula stretching from the mouth of the Murray River to Salt Creek, a distance of over 100 kilometres.

OPPOSITE BOTTOM: The main buildings of Mount Gambier, the commercial centre of the south-east, are made from locally quarried stone.

ABOVE: Larry the Lobster, in Kingston SE, welcomes visitors to the region.

LEFT: The blue water of Mount Gambier's Blue Lake looks almost artificial in its intensity. It is the only one of a series of local volcanic lakes to show this effect and the lake supplies much of the town's water without any visible change.

OPPOSITE: This local fisherman proudly shows off the morning's lobster catch.

TOP LEFT: The old Customs House next to the harbour must be one of the smallest ever built.

TOP RIGHT: The main street of Robe is lined with heritage listed buildings and looks like it must have done 100 years ago.

ABOVE: The harbour at Robe shelters the lobster fishing fleet and provides safe mooring for pleasure craft.

ABOVE: The sheltered coves of Little Dip National Park near Robe are only accessible by four-wheel-drive and are deserted much of the time—a great place for playing Robinson Crusoe.

LEFT: The home of the famous poet, Adam Lindsay Gordon, sits among beautiful native gardens near the seaside town of Port MacDonnell.

RIGHT: The pounding Southern Ocean has sculpted the soft rocks near Port MacDonnell into weird and wonderful shapes.

FOLLOWING PAGES: Red sandstone cliffs on the southern shore of Neapean Bay reflect the colours of a vivid sunset.

Kangaroo Island & the Fleurieu Peninsula

The Island

Kangaroo Island with its deserted beaches, wild coastline and national parks teeming with wildlife, is one of the best known parts of South Australia. It was also the first place in the state to be settled by migrants.

In 1802, Matthew Flinders made the first recorded visit here, at exactly the same time as French explorer Nicolas Baudin. Even though the two countries were at war at that time, the two ships put aside political differences and exchanged information on the region. Baudin returned the following summer and mapped out the south and west coastline. This explains the origin of French names, such as Cape du Couedic, Cape Gantheaume and Fleurieu Peninsula, that are seen on modern maps.

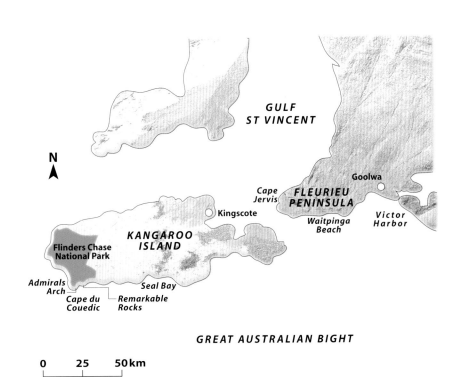

The first official settlers arrived in 1836 and founded Kingscote, the first free settlement. Originally designated to be state capital, its development was hampered by lack of water and timber. Eventually plans for this new settlement were abandoned in favour of the newly designed city of Adelaide.

The island quickly developed into a pastoral region with sheep being the main resource. Only recently has this situation changed, with the burgeoning tourism industry coming to the fore. Today, with the sheep industry at a low ebb, many farmers are doubling as Park Rangers to cope with the increasing pressures of tourism.

KI, as the locals call it, is a big island, a fact that takes many visitors by surprise when they head off to Flinders Chase National Park from Penneshaw. The island covers 4500 square kilometres and is 155 kilometres long, making it the third largest coastal island in the country. Much of the countryside is covered with rolling green hills, and with its quiet roads and neat little farms it has a delightfully pastoral feel.

A great attraction for visitors is the variety of wildlife, especially in the more remote south-western parts. Seal Bay is well known and is one of the few accessible sea lion colonies in the country. Each year 45000 people visit the colony and National Parks Guides conduct regular supervised walks to watch the seals at close quarters, and learn about their natural history. With this large number of visitors supervision is essential as the seals are mostly sleeping and feeding their young, exhausted after spending days hunting at sea.

Further along the coast, in the south-west corner, is another well-known part of the island, Flinders Chase National Park, which teems with kangaroos and possums. The park is well equipped for visitors and has a natural-style camping ground with full facilities at Rocky River. A totally fearless possum colony is an added bonus. Any evening, it is not unusual to find one of these delightful little furry creatures climbing up the leg of your trousers, looking for scraps of food. You may also find kangaroos in groups of three or four, following you around. It is best not to feed these animals, even though it is tempting, as they cannot digest our food, and they become so dependent on handouts that they stop looking for their proper foods. This has disastrous health consequences.

Down the coast at Cape du Couedic are the weird wind-sculpted shapes aptly called Remarkable Rocks, sitting isolated on a smooth rocky mound. This is a fascinating spot where orange-red lichen contrasts with blue skies, and where wild shapes of granite boulders seem too smooth to have been carved by nature's inexorable forces. The same powerful forces have hollowed out Admirals Arch right at the tip of the Cape. Here a boardwalk leads under huge overhangs, and New Zealand Fur Seals can be seen sunning themselves on the rocks far below, and swimming in the seething surf.

The Peninsula

Back across the water on the mainland, beyond Cape Jervis, is the Fleurieu Peninsula. It is a popular region for day trips out of Adelaide. The towns of Victor Harbor and Goolwa have become favourite spots for summer holidays, and some of the best surfing beaches in South Australia, such as Waitpinga Beach, are to be found along the southern coastline.

Victor Harbor is home to the well-known horse-drawn tram which travels across to Granite Island. This brightly painted double-decker wagon has become a kind of icon for the town. Nearby Goolwa, on the banks of the Murray River, has its own icon in the form of the steam powered Cockle Trains which run between the main towns in the area during the summer holidays.

The Fleurieu Peninsula is one of the most popular parts of the state, due not only to its handy distance from the city, but also to the variety of things to do. Even in the high season there are plenty of quiet places to escape from crowds, and the scenery, particularly along the south coast, is simply superb.

LEFT: The Lighthouse at Cape du Couedic.

OPPOSITE: Red lichen contrasts with the vivid blue sea at King George Beach on the north coast of Kangaroo Island.

RIGHT: Pelicans wait for their daily feed near the jetty in Kingscote.

BELOW RIGHT: The new Kangaroo Island ferry approaches the jetty at Cape Jervis on the mainland.

OPPOSITE: The road to Flinders Chase National Park passes miles of undisturbed bush on its way to Cape du Couedic.

OPPOSITE TOP AND ABOVE:
New Zealand Fur Seals in their
hundreds bask in the sun on
the rocks below Admirals Arch.

OPPOSITE BOTTOM: Seal Bay is one
of the few sea lion colonies that is
readily accessible. National Park
rangers conduct tours here to
observe the seals at close quarters
as they lie on the sand after
spending days at sea feeding.

RIGHT: Fairy Penguins inhabit the
coast at Penneshaw and can be
seen in the late evening as they
return from feeding.

BELOW RIGHT: Rosenberg's
Sand Goanna, seen near
Cape Willoughby lighthouse.

ABOVE AND OPPOSITE:
Remarkable Rocks near Cape du Couedic are aptly named, as the wind-sculpted rocks seemingly defy gravity. The intricate folds and smooth curves of these huge boulders are testament to the inexorable erosive powers of wind and rain over the eons.

ABOVE: The Corio Hotel in Goolwa near the mouth of the mighty Murray River.

LEFT AND FAR LEFT: The horse-drawn tram at Victor Harbor connects the mainland with Granite Island via a wooden causeway. The tram has become a kind of icon of the Fleurieu region.

ABOVE: Some of the best surf beaches in South Australia are to be found along the Peninsula's southern shore, like this one at Waitpinga Beach.

RIGHT: The old wharf at Goolwa is home to beautifully restored paddlesteamers. These stately craft used to be the main mode of transport to New South Wales along the Murray, but are now floating museums and pleasure steamers.

The author wishes to thank the following people and organisations

who very kindly helped with shooting the photographs for this book:

Peter Whitehead, Mammal Supervisor, Adelaide Zoo

Jon James, Opal Quest, Coober Pedy

John Reeves, Coober Pedy

Ken and Trish Ratford, Kay's House, Coober Pedy

Publican and staff at the William Creek Hotel

Steven Bourne at Naracoorte Caves

Hardy's Wines, McLaren Vale

Kay's Wines, McLaren Vale

Jim Barry Wines, Clare Valley

Eric Brand, Coonawarra

Mrs Clifford, Yallum Park, Penola

Loxton Historical Village

index

First published in Australia in 2000 by
New Holland Publishers (Australia) Pty Ltd
Sydney • Auckland • London • Cape Town
14 Aquatic Drive Frenchs Forest NSW 2086 Australia
218 Lake Road Northcote Auckland New Zealand
24 Nutford Place London W1H 6DQ United Kingdom
80 McKenzie Street Cape Town 8001 South Africa

National Library of Australia Cataloguing-in-Publication Data:

Rains, Nick.
South Australia.

Includes index.
ISBN 1 86436 562 5.

1. South Australia – Pictorial works. I. Title.

919.4230466

Publishing General Manager: Jane Hazell
Publisher: Averill Chase
Publishing Manager: Anouska Good
Project Editor: Sophie Church
Copy Editor: Alwyn Evans
Designed by: i2i design, Melanie Feddersen
Cartographer: Colin Seton
Reproduction: Colourscan
Printer: Kyodo Printing Co.

CAPTIONS

PAGE 2: Wheatfields near Burra; PAGE 4: Remarkable Rocks, Kangaroo Island; PAGE 8, TOP TO BOTTOM:
Robe Obelisk; Coonawarra grapes; Wedge-tailed Eagle; PAGE 9, TOP TO BOTTOM: North Adelaide;
resident of Kangaroo Island.

More of Nick Rains' superb photography can be viewed at www.nickrains.com.